GW01417352

To

_____

From

_____

_____

For Lewis and Dorian H.F.

Text by Lois Rock
Illustrations copyright © 2007 Hannah Firmin
This edition copyright © 2007 Lion Hudson
The moral rights of the author and illustrator
have been asserted

A Lion Children's Book
an imprint of
Lion Hudson plc
Mayfield House, 256 Banbury Road,
Oxford OX2 7DH, England
www.lionhudson.com
ISBN 978-0-7459-6045-6

First edition 2007
1 3 5 7 9 10 8 6 4 2 0
All rights reserved

Acknowledgments
All unattributed prayers are by Lois Rock copyright © Lion Hudson
Prayers by Sophie Piper and Victoria Tebbs are copyright © Lion Hudson
Bible extracts are taken or adapted from the Good News Bible, Published by The
Bible Societies/HarperCollins Publishers Ltd, UK and American Bible Society 1966,
1971, 1976, 1992 used by permission.
The Lord's Prayer from Common Worship: Services and Prayers for the Church of
England (Church House Publishing, 2000) is copyright © The English Language
Liturgical Consultation, 1988 and is reproduced by permission of the publishers.

A catalogue record for this book is available
from the British Library
Typeset in Venetian301 BT 15/18
Printed and bound in China

PRAYERS

for your

CONFIRMATION

Written and compiled by Lois Rock

Illustrated by Hannah Firmin

LION
CHILDREN'S

At confirmation, you make a promise to live the Christian life. At its heart are the two ancient commandments of which Jesus reminded his followers:

'Love the Lord your God with all your heart, with all your soul, and with all your mind.' 'Love your neighbour as you love yourself.'

The prayers in this book are given to encourage you in your walk of faith. They can help you find the words to ask God for strength and for blessing.

Worshipping God

O God, your greatness is seen in all the world!
I look at the sky, which you have made; at the
    moon and the stars, which you set in their
    places, and I wonder:
Who am I, that you think of me?
What is humankind, that you care for us?
O God, your greatness is seen in all the world!

From Psalm 8:1, 3–4

You are holy, Lord, the only God,
and your deeds are wonderful.

You are strong.
You are great.
You are the Most High,
You are almighty.
You, holy Father, are
King of heaven and earth.

You are Three and One,
Lord God, all good.
You are Good, all Good, supreme Good,
Lord God, living and true.

You are love,
You are wisdom.
You are humility,
You are endurance.
You are rest,
You are peace.
You are joy and gladness.
You are justice and moderation.

You are all our riches,
And you suffice for us.

You are beauty.
You are gentleness.

You are our protector,
You are our guardian and defender.
You are courage.
You are our haven and our hope.

You are our faith,
Our great consolation.
You are our eternal life,
Great and wonderful Lord,
God almighty,
Merciful Saviour.

St Francis of Assisi
(1181–1226)

You alone, O God, deserve praise and glory,
because of your constant love and faithfulness.

From Psalm 115:1

Our Lord and God! You are worthy
    to receive glory, honour and power.
For you created all things,
and by your will they were given
    existence and life.

Revelation 4:11

Honour God, and praise
    his greatness!
Worship him who made
    heaven, earth, sea,
and the springs of water!

Words of the Angel of Good News,
Revelation 14:7

May none of God's wonderful works keep silence,
night or morning. Bright stars, high mountains,
the depths of the seas, sources of rushing rivers:
may all these break into song as we sing to Father,
Son and Holy Spirit. May all the angels in the
heavens reply: Amen, Amen, Amen. Power, praise,
honour, eternal glory to God, the only Giver of
grace, Amen, Amen, Amen.

Anonymous (3rd –6th centuries)

Since he is wise he loves you with wisdom.
Since he is good he loves you with goodness.
Since he is holy he loves you with holiness.
Since he is just he love you with justice.
Since he is merciful he loves you with mercy.
Since he is compassionate he loves you with
   compassion.
Since he is gentle he loves you with gentleness.

St John of the Cross (1542–91)

O God,
as truly as you are our father,
so just as truly you are our mother.
We thank you, God our father,
for your strength and goodness.
We thank you, God our mother,
for the closeness of your caring.
O God, we thank you for the great love
you have for each one of us.

Julian of Norwich (1342–after 1416)

There is no place where God is not –
wherever I go, there God is.
Now and always he upholds me with his power
and keeps me safe in his love.

Anonymous

Who may come into God's presence?

The person who obeys God in everything,
who always speaks the truth,
who keeps every promise,
who cannot be lured into doing wrong.

Such a person will be safe all through life.

From Psalm 15

Do not follow the advice of the wicked,
but obey every word of God.

For the wicked are nothing more than wisps
of straw in the autumn gale; but the righteous
are like trees that grow by the life-giving river,
bearing leaves and fruit in their season.

From Psalm 1

Lord,
Help me to live this day
Quietly, easily.
Help me to lean upon Thy
Great strength
Trustfully, restfully,
To wait for the unfolding
Of Thy will
Patiently, serenely,
To meet others
Peacefully, joyously,
To face tomorrow
Confidently, courageously.
Amen.

St Francis of Assisi (1181–1226)

O Lord,
I have heard your laws.
May I worship you.
May I worship you alone.
May all I say and do show respect for your holy
name.
May I honour the weekly day of rest.
May I show respect for my parents.
May I reject violence so that I never take a life.
May I learn to be loyal in friendship and so learn
to be faithful in marriage.
May I not steal what belongs to others.
May I not tell lies to destroy another person's
reputation.
May I not be envious of what others have, but
may I learn to be content with the good things
you give me.

Based on the Ten Commandments, Exodus 20

O God, make me good.
Make me wise.
Make me hardworking.
Make me honest.
Make me tactful.
Make me generous.
Make me truthful.
Make me loyal.
But most of all,
dear God,
make me your child.

Based on Proverbs

Take my wrongdoing
and throw it away,
down in the deep of the sea;
welcome me into your kingdom of love
for all of eternity.

Based on Micah 7:18–20

God, have pity on me, a sinner!

*From Jesus' parable of the Pharisee
and the tax collector, Luke 18:13*

From the mud
a pure white flower

From the storm
a clear blue sky

As we pardon
one another

God forgives us
from on high.

Sophie Piper

I told God everything:
I told God about all the wrong things I had done.
I gave up trying to pretend.
I gave up trying to hide.
I knew that the only thing to do was to confess.

And God forgave me.

Based on Psalm 32:5

Following Jesus

The seed is Christ's,
The harvest is Christ's;
In the granary of God
May we be gathered.

The sea is Christ's,
The fishes are Christ's;
In the nets of God
May we all meet.

Irish Prayer

Dear God,
May I set my heart on the things that are of
eternal value.
May they be to me more than any other treasure.
May I be part of your kingdom.

Based on Matthew 6:33

Dear God,
May I find shelter in your
kingdom, just as the birds of
the air find shelter in a tree.

Based on the parable of the mustard seed,
Matthew 13:31–32

Dear God,
I am your lost sheep.
Please find me.
Please take me home.

Based on the parable of the lost sheep,
Luke 15

Dear God,
Help me to listen to what you have to say to me.
May the Evil One not snatch the message away.
May troubles not cause me to stop following you.
May worrying about material things not choke out
  my longing for holiness.
May I grow and flourish in your kingdom.

Based on the parable of the sower, Matthew 13:1–24

My candle burns; its tiny light
shines to make this dark place bright.

My candle burns, a flame of love,
shining up to heaven above.

Anonymous

Help me, Lord, to show your love.
Help me to be patient and kind, not jealous
or conceited or proud.
May I never be ill-mannered, selfish or irritable;
may I be quick to forgive and forget.
May I not gloat over wrongdoing, but rather be
glad about things that are good and true.
May I never give up loving: may my faith and
hope and patience never come to an end.

Based on 1 Corinthians 13:4 –7

Love is giving, not taking,
mending, not breaking,
trusting, believing,
never deceiving
patiently bearing
and faithfully sharing
each joy, every sorrow,
today and tomorrow.

Anonymous

Lord, make me an instrument of your peace.
Where there is hatred, let me sow love;
Where there is injury, pardon;
Where there is discord, union;
Where there is doubt, faith;
Where there is despair, hope;
Where there is darkness, light;
Where there is sadness, joy.

O divine Master, grant that I may not so
much seek to be consoled as to console, to
be understood as to understand, to be loved
as to love; for it is in giving that we receive,
it is in pardoning that we are pardoned, and
it is in dying that we are born to eternal life.

Attributed to St Francis of Assisi

(1181–1226)

Our Father in heaven:
May your holy name be honoured;
may your Kingdom come;
may your will be done on earth as it is in heaven.
Give us today the food we need.
Forgive us the wrongs we have done,
as we forgive the wrongs that others have done
    to us.
Do not bring us to hard testing,
but keep us safe from the Evil One.

Matthew 6:9 –13

Father:
May your holy name be honoured;
may your kingdom come.
Give us day by day the food we need.
Forgive us our sins,
for we forgive everyone who does us wrong.
And do not bring us to hard testing.

Luke 11:2–4

Our Father in heaven,
hallowed be your name,
your kingdom come,
your will be done,
on earth as in heaven.
Give us today our daily bread.
Forgive us our sins
as we forgive those who sin against us.
Lead us not into temptation
but deliver us from evil.

For the kingdom, the power,
and the glory are yours
now and for ever.
Amen.

The Lord's Prayer

Lord Jesus:
Be the way in which I walk.
Be the truth that makes me wise.
Be the life that brings me safely into God's
  presence.

Based on John 14:6

Jesus, who walked to the cross,
be with us when we feel abandoned.

Jesus, who walked to the cross,
be with us when we face danger.

Jesus, who walked to the cross,
be with us when we are suffering.

When wickedness threatens to defeat us,
Jesus, who rose from the dead, be with us.

We celebrate Easter with the disciples who saw the risen Jesus, and who knew that love was stronger than death.

We also remember Thomas, for whom Easter was a long time coming, and all those who feel alone in their doubt and despair.

Risen Jesus, make yourself known to us all in due time so we may know for sure the joy of heaven.

Living
in the Spirit

I am a pilgrim
on a journey
to the place
where God is found;
every step
along that journey
is upon
God's holy ground.

Open my mind, O Lord,
to see your light.

Open my mind, O Lord,
to know the hope to which you have called me.

Open my mind, O Lord,
to see the wonderful blessings you have promised.

Open my mind, O Lord,
to see your power at work in me.

Based on Ephesians 1:18-19

May everything I do be a sacrament to gentleness
A step to the horizon land of white and gold
A seed that I sow in the earth of everlastingness
Reaching up to heaven as its leaves unfold.

Spirit of God, put love in my life.
Spirit of God, put joy in my life.
Spirit of God, put peace in my life.

Spirit of God, make me patient.
Spirit of God, make me kind.
Spirit of God, make me good.

Spirit of God, give me faithfulness.
Spirit of God, give me humility.
Spirit of God, give me self-control.

From Galatians 5:22–23

Lord, make this house
a holy place
filled with your love
and heaven's grace.

Dear God, bless those who visit us: family,
friends and strangers. May we make our home
a place of love and kindness for all. May we
share the things we have with generosity and
cheerfulness.

Victoria Tebbs

Dear God,
Guard our friendships:

Encourage us,
that we may encourage one another.

Inspire us,
that we may inspire one another.

Strengthen us,
that we may strengthen one another.

Remember us,
that we may remember one another.

Sophie Piper

Father God,
Gather us all into a circle of friendship
and circle us about with your love.

Sophie Piper

O God,
We are all strangers in this world
and we are all travelling to the eternal country.

So may we not treat anyone as
a foreigner or an outsider,
but simply as a fellow human being
made in your image.

We share the earth
we share the sky
we share the shining sea
with those we trust
with those we fear:
we are God's family.

May we learn to appreciate different
points of view:

to know that the view from the hill is
    different from the view in the valley;
the view to the east is different from
    the view to the west;
the view in the morning is different
    from the view in the evening;
the view of a parent is different from
    the view of a child;
the view of a friend is different from
    the view of a stranger;
the view of humankind is different from
    the view of God.

May we all learn to see what is good,
what is true, what is worthwhile.

Dear God,
Give us the courage to
overcome anger with love.

God our Father, Creator of the world,
please help us to love one another.
Make nations friendly with other nations;
make all of us love one another like brothers
  and sisters.
Help us to do our part to bring peace in
  the world
and happiness to all people.

Prayer from Japan

O God,
Settle the quarrels among the nations.

May they hammer their swords into ploughs
and their spears into pruning knives…

Where the tanks now roll, let there be tractors;
where the landmines explode, let the fields grow
    crops.

Let there be a harvest of fruit and grain
and peace that all the world can share.

Based on Micah 4:3–5

Heal the world's sorrows
Dry the world's tears
Calm the world's worries
End the world's fears.

Our world is fallen
as if from heaven.

Our world is broken
so we shall mend it.

Our world is wounded
so we shall heal it.

Our world is the Lord's
and God will bless it.

God has not promised a world without
sorrow; but God has promised to be
with us in our sorrow.

Come, O Joy:
Let heaven break into my dark night
of sorrow like the early dawn of
a summer morning.

May the world turn round about,
may all things turn to right;
may the sunset thank the dawn,
the noontime bless the night;

May the rivers thank the rain,
the storm clouds bless the sea;
may the good soil thank the leaves,
the sunshine bless the tree;

May the rich thank those in need,
the children bless the old;
may the strong thank those who fail,
the timid bless the bold;

May the angels sing on earth,
may heaven hear our prayer;
may forgiveness, joy and peace
and love fill everywhere.

Thank you, dear God, for marking out our years
with the pattern of the seasons: with leaves
unfolding, flowers blooming, seeds falling,
new life in the dark earth waiting.

As the rain hides the stars, as the autumn mist
hides the hills, as the clouds veil the blue of the
sky, so the dark happenings of my lot hide the
shining of your face from me. Yet, if I may hold
your hand in the darkness, it is enough. Since I
know that, though I may stumble in my going,
you do not fall.

Gaelic prayer (translated by Alistair MacLean)

Dear God, you are my shepherd,
You give me all I need,
You take me where the grass grows green
And I can safely feed.

You take me where the water
Is quiet and cool and clear;
And there I rest and know I'm safe
For you are always near.

From Psalm 23

Kind Jesus,
Welcome us to the room you
have made ready for us.
Wash us clean from the
dust of the journey.
Bless us as we share the
bread and wine.

Be thou a bright flame before me,
Be thou a guiding star above me,
Be thou a smooth path below me,
And be a kindly shepherd behind me,
Today, tonight, and for ever.

From Carmina Gadelica